God's Perfectly Awesome Idea

WRITTEN BY **Claudia West**
ILLUSTRATED BY **Elettra Cudignotto**

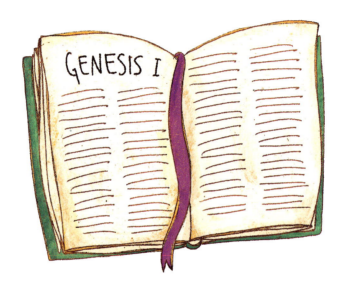

God's Perfectly Awesome Idea

Copyright © 2021 by Claudia West
Illustration copyright © 2021 by Elettra Cudignotto
All rights reserved.

No part of this book may be reproduced or transmitted in any form or by any means, electronic or mechanical, including photocopying, recording, or by any information storage and retrieval system, without permission in writing from the publisher.

Heyer Publishing
GrammyGiggles.com | Claudia@GrammyGiggles.com

Library of Congress Control Number: data on file
ISBN: 978-1-7338784-2-5

Book Consultant: Judith Briles, The Book Shepherd, The Book Shepherd.com
Cover and interior design, eBook conversion : Rebecca Finkel, F + P Graphic Design, FPGD.com

Printed in United States of America

Dedicated to Adley Jack
a Grammy Giggles Super Fan

"For every child, everywhere...
Because God loves each one!"
— Grammy Giggles

It was dark, oh so dark.
It must've been dark.
Before Genesis One
it was dark dark DARK.

God sat on His throne.
He sat all alone.
But what fun is a throne
if you're sitting alone?

Nothing to play with!
Too dark to see!
No mountains, no cities,
not even a tree!
No PUPPIES! No KITTIES!
No Life had begun.
Do you think it was fun
before Genesis One?

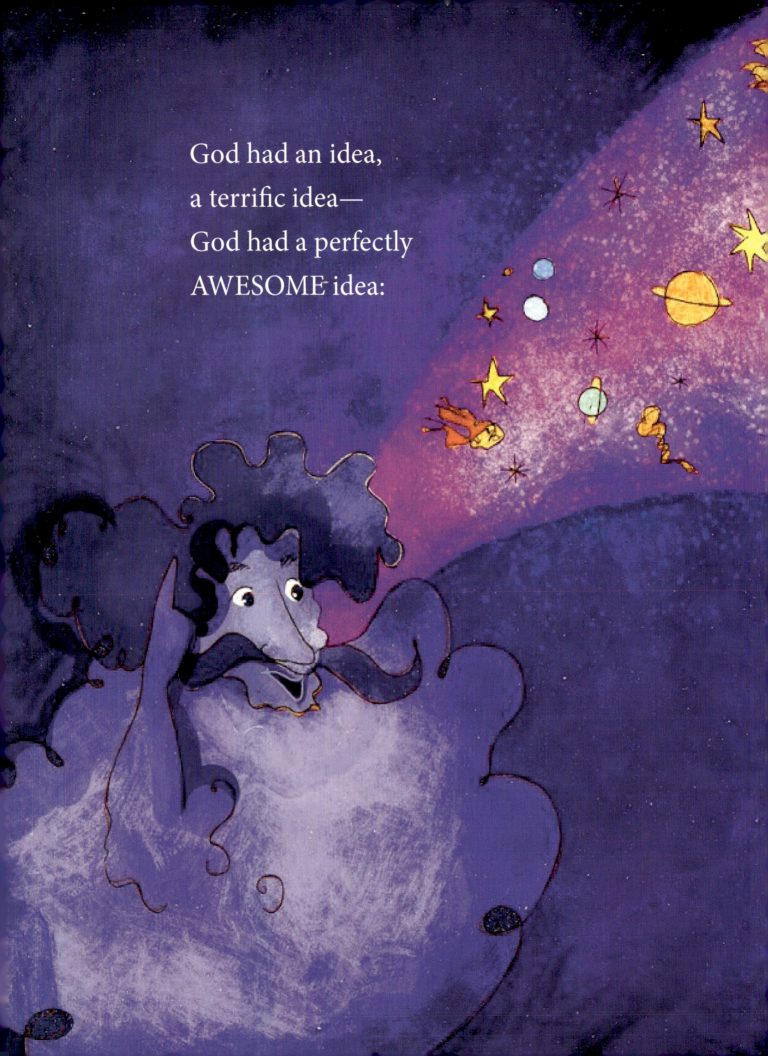

"I'll fix up a planet
with everything on it!
I'll have a big universe,
moon, stars, and comets,
bright sun, fluffy clouds,
red sunsets, green trees,
huge mountains, deep valleys,
and fishes in seas!"

Ideas kept coming:
"I'll have horses that run!
Yes, horses that run
will be OODLES of fun!
And the best thing of all
that I've planned in my Plan:
(it's SUPER COLOSSAL!!)
I'll create a MAN!"
When He'd planned out His plans
and He knew they were right,
He said, as He started,

And oh!
What a light!
So bright!
What a sight!
The light separated
the day from the night.
From dark of the night
to light of the day
the light just pushed
all of the darkness away.
And that was the start
of the very first day!

God said to Himself
On day number two—
"On day number two
I know just what to do.
I'll make a blue sky
above water so blue!"

The bluest of days
was that day number two.
That day number two was
truly true blue.

On day number three
He made land for the trees.
He made plants for all uses
and trees out of wood.
They looked as they should.

The fourth day He made
The sun, stars, and moon.
The sunlight He made
not a moment too soon!
The plants needed sunlight to grow,
so did trees.

God saw that it worked well
And God was SO pleased!

On day number five
He made all things alive
in the seas and the skies
on day number five.
He just spoke the words
And made fishes and birds:
"I'd like starfish and sharks
and clown fish and carps,
big whales with big tails
and small shells on small snails
and parakeets, eagles,
toucans, and magpies
to swim in the oceans
or fly in the skies."

And that was enough for day number five.

There was much to complete
The sixth day of the week:
He made all the animals, both great and small.
(He made up so many I can't count them all!)
He made elephants, zebras, and lions with ease
He just spoke the word and
He made chimpanzees,
and the ducks and the cows
and the piggies and lambs...

And, oh yes, He made those wild horses that ran!

And then the LORD came
to the star of his plan:
on that sixth day of days
God fashioned a man.
The man was named Adam—
the only man there.
He could pet all the beasts
without worry or care.

Then God said to Adam,
"You looked all alone,
so while you were sleeping
I took a rib bone.
And from one of your ribs
I made you a wife—
a woman named Eve
to love your whole life."

Made in God's image,
they looked as they should.
God looked at His work
And He said,
"THIS is GOOD!"

On day number seven
God looked down from Heaven.
He'd made everything best—
today He would rest.

And that is the story
of how Life was begun.
It's all written down
in

Grammy Giggles says,

Now you may be thinking
it's too great a feat
to make all this cool stuff
in less than a week!
How long would it take YOU
to make just one flower?
Three years or ten days—
you think maybe one hour?

I think if I gave you
a lifetime to try it
you'd have to give up
and go out and just buy it!
But God is so GREAT
that He just spoke the Word,
and things were created
when that Word was heard!

If He can do that
Then you know it is true
That God will always
Be there for YOU…

And think of how cool
That before Time began
In God's mind you were there
As the Star of His Plan!

Parents' Page

Did God really do this is only 6 days — 144 hours?

Scholars have studied this for centuries and have taken a stand on both sides. The Hebrew word for "day" in Genesis 1 is "yowm" and can be translated: a) sunrise to sunset, b) sunset to sunset, (c) segment of time, d) age or epoch. I believe that whether Creation happened in a week or multiple millennia (or somewhere in-between), we can all agree that it doesn't change the awesome creativity and power of God when "He just spoke the Word and things were created when that Word was heard". The Hebrew word for creation is "bara," meaning "out of nothing." He did not clone His creation from something; He made it out of nothing.

Is this what God really looks like?

No, this GodCloud is just a fun representation of God. In the Old Testament, God told Moses in Exodus 33:20: *"You cannot see My face."* In the New Testament, I John 4:12 says, *"No one has ever seen God."* However, He sent Jesus so that we could "see" what God is like. Hebrews 1:3 tells us that Jesus is *"the reflection of God's glory and the exact imprint of His being." (All scriptures from the NRSV.)*

Adam and Eve were the Stars of His creation!

They were given total authority and dominion, like royalty, over the earth with all its plants and animals, to use it, to explore it, to take care of it. (See Genesis 1:26, 28) Humans still have this royal authority and responsibility. Why? Because they were made in God's image. When we choose to follow God, we become part of that same Royal Family!

Made in Gods image

People do not all look alike, so what does "made in God's image" mean? Those who believe in God have His Holy Spirit living in them, which enables them to reflect the glory and nature of God. In the same way, when we look in the mirror, we should see a reflection of God's glory! In the Old Testament, Isaiah 60:2: *"His glory will be seen upon you"* (ESV). In the New Testament, 2 Corinthians 3:18: *"We see the glory of the Lord as though reflected in a mirror, and we are being transformed into the same image"* (NRSV). How does the Spirit transform us into God's nature? In the Old Testament, Isaiah 11:2 says that the Spirit teaches us wisdom, understanding, counsel, knowledge, reverence of God, right and just judgment. In the New Testament, Galatians 5:22-23 tells us these are evidences of the Holy Spirit working in our lives: love, joy, peace, patience, kindness, goodness, faithfulness, gentleness, and self-control. Because humans can have God's spirit living in them, share His attributes, have free will, and can make decisions not governed by instinct, they are distinctly different from the rest of creation, that is: made in His image.

Full disclosure: Genesis 2

There are two parts of this story that are actually taken from the next chapter in Genesis. Genesis 2:2 says that on the seventh day God rested from all the work He had done. Genesis 2:21-22 explains how God took one of Adam's rib bones to make Eve.

Claudia West
also known as **Grammy Giggles**

Inspired by Dr. Seuss' books, she wrote a series of memorable and fun Bible stories when her two daughters, Rachel and Hannah, were little. Oodles of years drifted by, and her stories just sat, sat, sat on her computer. Now her granddaughter calls her Grammy and the kids at the Royal Family KIDS Camp call her Giggles. All love her stories as they sit, sit, sit listening and laughing. Now you can do the same with her Grammy Giggles' Bible stories.

Calling Colorado home, she loves the beach when she vacations, enjoying the sights and sounds of the sea.

GrammyGiggles.com
Claudia@GrammyGiggles.com

Elettra Cudignotto
with her dog Giungla

Elettra lives in Vicenza, Italy and studied art at "IUAV" in Venice where in 2012 she graduated in Visual Arts and in 2014 she obtained a master degree in Economics and Management of Arts at "Ca Foscari."

She is talented in many genres of art, and specializes in book illustration. All her work is done in digital but her goal is to keep her drawings as much rough as possible because she loves textures, brushes, vivid colours and irregular lines.

To view more of her artwork and to contact her visit:

www.ElettraCudignotto.com

The Zoo on the Sea

Noah was probably ready to take life easy when God chose him as the Man for His Big and Wet Plan. Grammy Giggles asks kids lots of questions to think about as Noah prepares for a Big Flood, as well as what went on in the Ark for a year! Grammy Giggles is glad that Noah saved all the animals for us to enjoy!

Fish Tummy Soup

Told from the Fish's point of view, we learn about a happy fish who was minding his own business when God sent him on a mission. Just what was that secret mission? What happened when the Fish did his job? Grammy Giggles thinks that good things happen when people and fishes use their talents to do what God has in mind.

The Very Scary Pajama Drama

Daniel was a really good guy, but some really bad guys made sure he was arrested in his pajamas to go bunk with very hungry lions for the night. The next morning the King was in *his* pajamas as he ran to see if Daniel survived the Pajama Drama. Grammy Giggles wonders: Did the Lions listen to God or to their grumbly tummies?

There are many more stories to come! Discover them all!

Profits from the sales of this book will be donated to RFK.org

Praise for

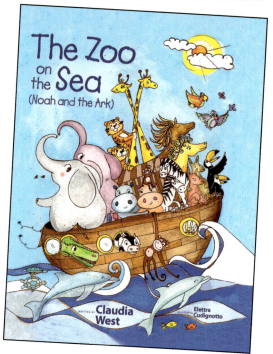

Grammy Giggles has written a charming book that children will love, giving a child's-eye view of the Bible story Noah and the Ark. Your child will delight in the colorful, engaging illustrations and will thoroughly enjoy the rhyming text. I highly recommend this captivating book.
—**JoAnn Wagner,** author *Sir Pigglesworth's* Children's book series

This text is fantastic! Really. It's so fun to read and the cadence and tone are just perfect for children. I'm so impressed! (And I've reviewed many, many children's books.) All in all, it's absolutely wonderful and totally appropriate for children of any faith.
—**Linda Loewenstein,** freelance editor

This story of Noah and his ark is biblically accurate and yet told by author Claudia West in a whimsical and fun rhyming manner. The artwork is cheerful and enticing, too!   —**K. K. Newman,** teacher

The Zoo on the Sea is a brilliant retelling of the Biblical account of Noah and the Ark. Children will love the rhyme, the story, and the colorful, creative pictures. Grammy Giggles has created a book that will become a favorite for many children.
—**Janet Brannberg,** teacherelementary and special education

I love reading rhyming books to kids when they are well done and this one is very well done. The story is accurate and a great way for kids to learn the story of Jonah and the whale!... Illustrations are first rate and a quality book.
—**Lisa Reinicke,** multi-award winning author, speaker, and coach

Praise for

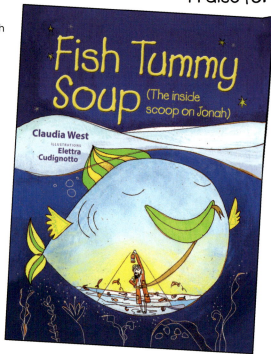

I am a past elementary school teacher and appreciate the well written story and colorful pictures. But more importantly as a grandparent my grandchildren absolutely love both of Claudia's books. They love the rhymes, the colorful pictures and the story lines. Definitely a must buy for every family of small children!   —**Rebecca Matson**

Fish Tummy Soup is absolutely wonderful! Grammy Giggles does an amazing job of making Bible stories come to life with engaging cadence and beautiful illustrations. Her books have quickly become favorites. Highly recommend!   —**Whitney Lott**

After loving Claudia's first book The Zoo on the Sea, I was anxious to see what else she would surprise us with. Fish Tummy Soup is just as whimsical, especially to read out loud. The rhymes are delightful… Nice new telling of age-old Bible Stories for our times.   —**Pam Allen**